The Other Side of the Door

Volume 1: Reflections

By: Etrec J. White

iWrite4orU Publishing
PO Box 551006
Jacksonville, FL 32255
www.iwrite4oru.com

Printed in the United States of America

Genre: Poetry

ISBN: 978-0-692-56928-3

Connect with Author Etrec J. White:

www.Facebook.com/EtrecJWhite

Instagram | Twitter: @CERTEfiedPOETRY

Table of Contents

Dedication

This book is dedicated to Mr. Randy M. Thomas. I have learned so much from you, whether it was from insightful conversations, or sitting back watching you conduct yourself in a business manner. You helped mold me into the man that I am today, and I am so grateful to have you in my corner. I've learned that when you meet genuinely true people, you latch on to them and become a sponge, soaking up all of the knowledge they possess. Thank you for helping me become a better father, a better son, a better friend, and a better person. Through many of my trials you have always been right there. Helping me to stay focused was a tough task, but me saying *thank you* is just a small piece of what you mean to me. Most of all, thank you for being my friend and mentor!

Acknowledgments

First and foremost, I give God all of the praises and honor, for blessing me with this trait He has bestowed upon me. For that, I will continuously say thank you!

I would like to say thank you to my wonderful parents, who always support me. My mother, Melba Dale; Dorthea White; and my father Hayward White. Thank you for each life lesson you have taught me. The Harris family and the Greene family, I love you all deeply. My Aunts, Uncles, and Cousins. R.I.P to my Grandfather, Wilburn Harris, and Barbara Greene. I love you and miss you both so much!

To my wonderful daughter, Elysha White, thank you for making me a better man. As you grow, I grow, and we grow together! Thank you for being simply amazing and continue to be creative, I love you so much! —Daddy

To my brothers: Elliot White, Christopher Dale, and Richard Scott. Thank you for always being there and helping support my dreams! Love you all.

To those who keep me grounded and humbled, and support me unconditionally, I say thank you, too:

My church family: Southside C.O.G.I.C; Patricia Brown; Chris Davis (and family); Samuel Mueller; Rachel Stewart; Ronnie White; Rico and LaSharon Zamor; Sophia Campbell (and family); Tiffany Taylor; Tomika Rodall; Brian Johnson (and family); Kevin Vasser (and family); Maxine Alexander (and family); Marvin Seyki; Christopher Andrews; Kimberly Hardy; LeAnna Rice; Takeysha Webster (and family); Corey Hart; Tychell J. Clark; Anthony Houston; LaRonda Felton; Dennis Lewis (and family); David Jackson (and family); Mark Royal; Juron Dicks; Andrea Arnette; LaTonia Stephens; Lorenzo Holiday; Terrance Nixon; Shana Lester; Nicole Thomas; Shanna Hodge; LaToya Joyner; Dre Spears (and family); Mandi Dyer (and family); Eddie Baker; Stephanie Smith; Samuel Peery (and family); Tredina Graham; My other Parents: Andre and Rita Austin (and family); Jannelle and Andre Tyus (and family); Sam and Ashley Miller; Jurell Hill (and family); Travis Hemphill; Anitra Jackson.

Thank you to all those who have read the pieces I put together, and have given all of the wonderful feedback. I didn't write to touch anyone, but I'm glad that so many have let me know how my writing has touched and affected them. So, I say thank you again!

Notes from the Desk

Scribbling, Scrambling, Doodling,
I'm thinking about…

With You (Elysha S. White)

With you
Is the best place to be!
With you
Is where I want to be!
Actually,
Where I need to be!

To touch your pretty face,
Or feel your touch
Makes my heart race!

I love you so much
You are everything to me
Lovely,
Beautiful,
You are wonderful to me,

With you,
No, for you.

When you are down,
and I'm around
That frown will be upside down!
I can't help but to look
at you and smile
Wipe the tears from
My eyes
As I thank God
For such a wonderful child!

I know you love your mom,
But, you are also a daddy's girl
My most precious gift

In the whole wide world!
With you
I close my eyes
For the best wishes
With you
I want to be near
I love your kisses!

I can say it a thousand times
I love you,
But the best place to be
Is clearly…
With you!

School Daze

I was scared to tell you how I really felt
Seeing you walk by me in school,
My heart would melt
Yeah, there were females
That really liked me
But, you and me
sounded good
And was suitable

It took a long time for me to get my nerves up
Truthfully, I was always scared
Of getting my feelings hurt
I would write you letter after letter,
and seeing who you were dating,
I knew you could do better
That is, if you were with me
so you could see that other side,
Everyone else was dying to see

I'm older now,
But you never left my mind
I still think about you,
And somehow smile
Imagining if you were mine
Wondering, if we could still be together,
Or am I a couple of steps behind?

If I am,
it would be so hurtful,
What I have is so personal,
And these feelings are irreversible

That school version of me is long gone,

and I've been told that
you're not ready for a relationship,
'cause you have been done
So wrong

I can relate!

I've experienced heartache,
but to get with you,
I wouldn't hesitate
I would take things slow
You would experience true love,
And that, I know

I was scared to tell you how I was feeling
My fault, blame my adrenaline
Not a rush,
Past a crush,
Being with you,
was always something that I desired too much

If it's meant to be,
Then maybe one day
we can cross paths
and share something more
than old school stories
and silly laughs

We can share our hearts

Reflection (To My Dad)

I'm looking in the mirror,
and I hate what's in front of my eyes!
I'm so mad
I want to break down and cry
The more I look at me,
I see you
and the more I admit it,
I'm just like you

I look just like you!
The things that I've been through,
are similar to you,
And what you've been through
I never wanted to be like you!
'cause deep down inside my heart,
I hated you!

Instead of changing,
I followed your footsteps,
and did half of the things,
That you would do!
Yeah, you're cool
and that's me in a sense,
but even though there's similarity
There is a major difference!

I'm not going to talk down,
Or even discredit you
That's not me
Plus, I love you
There are just some things
that I have to get off my chest,
and I can't talk to you,

So, this route was best
You never came to many of my games,
and my friends thought you were so cool,
But, I was ashamed!
Actually, it was more of an embarrassment
'cause all you did was bicker
And did that harassment shit!

All I wanted was your support,
and for you to tell me that you loved me,
and no matter how right or wrong I was,
That you got me
Nope, I would get cussed out
Or you'd get rowdy
My feelings inside,
I'd hide
It had nothing to do with pride
Just some things I put to the side
Locked away;
and never hoped to find!

I'm cold and nonchalant because of you!
I've taken the worse, most harsh words
The majority of them came from you!
I had to put my feelings in check,
'cause you were my dad,
though it was the case,
I would never disrespect!
Everything you have done and said though,
I will never forget!

We bump heads,
because we are so much alike
Seeing you is the reflection of seeing me,
And I guess that's why we drive each other crazy!

I know out of all my siblings,
I'm the rebel
The black sheep...
All the hurtful things,
They don't get to me
I ignore them

You see, you fuel my fire!
My anger and rage,
I turn into desire
To be better
And I'm willing to do what it takes
However...
Whenever...
Whatever...

You didn't know that I was as good as I was in ball
Or that I even had a poetic side
That's your fault
I told you there was so much more to me,
than "Pretty Boy" looks
Somebody who can dress
And loves to cook

I'm affectionate
Full of passion
A sports junkie
Someone who loves action
Most of all
Someone who loves his dad
Reaching out for his love,
That's all I've ever wanted to have

Someone to help me,
And show me how to be a dad

I'm no longer mad
This is just something I have to grow through,
but at the end of the day,
Just know that I still love you!

I may not talk to you for months or even years
If something happened to you
and I never told you how I felt
Would be my biggest fear!

So, I'll tell you now,
well, not really tell you,
But, write it down
I'll put my anger to the side,
'cause I love you to life
Always,
Your son,
Etrec Jamel White

To Whom It May Concern

To whom it may concern,
Thank you so much
for breaking me and my fiancée's heart!
For tearing it up,
Stepping on it,
Crushing it!

Thank you for all the disrespect,
And all the little subliminal messages that you sent
To get under our skin
All the heartache and sleepless nights
To the point where,
There were many nights I had to cry myself to sleep
Thank you for pushing not only me,
But us from love,
So you thought!

For making me bitter,
Turning my heart cold and sour
To where I couldn't stand the thought,
Or even the taste of love

Thank you for making me
Heartless and full of rage,
To the point and brink of where
I almost would lose my cool
On the edge!

Thank you for being so annoying to my fiancée
And making her disappointed and sad,
Thank you for making her disgusted,
To the point where she didn't even want
To think about opening up her heart,

And allowing someone to come into her life,
To prove that real love does exist!

See, you are being thanked because
You thought when you left and did all
Of the childish things you did
That we would just throw in the towel,
Quit,
Just give up
And for so long that was the case,
But you pushed us,
Motivated us,
Actually,
You pushed us closer to each other

Because for so long,
I was being blinded by the fact of loving somebody else
I thought no one could understand
The hurt and pain I was feeling
But, somebody did
She experienced some of the same pain
Which made it easier for me to open up
And communicate

Expressed how I felt
Put my cards on the table,
And played the hand I was dealt

Thank you for thinking we were washed up,
And that the right person wouldn't come along,
Because to the contrary, the right person did
Come along
And it's the one that you did wrong,
Who is actually right, well, perfect for me

To whom this may concern,
Thank you for bringing me and my baby together,
Because, all the negativity that you thought
You created,
You actually turned into a positive energy;
You made us more humble,
And more appreciative of each other
You turned something so small into something
Huge and enormous

Thank you for bringing me and my fiancée together,
Off of a technicality that just didn't seem right to you
We both want to thank you
All
All of you for the hurt,
Aggravation and pain,
And though every day isn't a perfect day for us,
We are perfect together
So, this is a lesson learned,
We just wanted to thank you personally,
Me and my fiancée

To whom it may concern

Maiysha

The first time I saw you,
I thought to myself how beautiful you were,
and how I had to have you in my life
You were a breath of fresh air
That some way,
By any means
I had to capture
And have in my world

The more we talked and started,
To get to know one another
Things began to reveal themselves
I knew that in such a short time,
you'd be the one I would
Feel safe giving my heart to

Look you eye to eye
While face to face
And say:
I love you

It was more than puppy love;
It was true genuine feelings
More than emotions…

Then we started dating and everything was fine
I was the happiest person,
so glad that you were mine
on cloud 9

Couldn't wait to see you every day
Just to give you comfort,
Because I knew that you were dealing with so much

And the more I saw you
And paid attention
You weren't all that tough

You were sweet
A real sweetheart indeed
I loved writing your name next to mine
It looked just as good as you and I being together
Somewhere down the line
Our communication went astray
No matter what,
I still stayed eager
So many thoughts in my head,
All I want to do is please her!

Kissing your soft, beautiful lips
While closing my eyes
In a peaceful bliss
I don't know what happened
I wanted to make things last
Our arguments just weren't worth it
Couldn't make things perfect
With you

Time has passed
But when I think of you,
Maiysha,
My beautiful…
Lovely…
Pretty…
Friend…
This is what comes to mind

Thoughts of the "Hills"

I loved being around your family
Inside I felt some jealousy
because you all were so perfect to me
I know that everyone has
their own problems,
but loving your daughter,
and being part of your family,
Was something I wanted

It wasn't just for show
It was receiving that much love from you all
So, deep down it was a lesson taught
To me
That I should value everything
and hold dearest things
Close to me

I know that I'm young,
but this is the closest thing
to the Huxtables
that I will ever see

You made me feel comfortable
when I came around,
except for that one time;
When we had that talk,
and you told me if
I was to ever hurt your daughter
that you will hunt me down
That actually gave me chill bumps
A tingly sensation up my spine
which made me stay on top of my game

I didn't want to run nor hide
It was a sense of pride
Respect
and whether you know it or not,
it was something I could never forget

I have a daughter now,
so I totally understand
what you meant
and where you were coming from
Because it's going to be a problem
If someone ever does my daughter wrong

I just wanted you to know that I appreciate you
and your family
and seeing your daughter's heart smile
is all that matters to me

I love you all, too.

Something for the "Hills"

Demiah

You're gone now
I never had the chance or opportunity to say sorry
I took advantage of you and your feelings
Never really thought you loved me
Like you said you did
I was just full of pride
Too proud to admit that I felt
the way you did

Yes, we were young
All the arguments
were overshadowed by wonderful moments
Despite
What I said or did,
I know that if you were here,
I would be with you
having you as my wife

But, my immaturity made you
Take your life
It haunts me in the worst way
No matter how hard I try
POW!
It's loud
An echoing sound
in my ear,
a sudden silence,
I feel the tears,
I can't believe you are not here
I carry that burden deep in my heart

I've never told anyone about the true love
That I lost

A lot of quiet times,
I'm thinking of you
I guess that is one reason why
I have ice in my veins

I've opened up my heart
to let some of this pain out
Saying I'm sorry is all that
had to come out of my mouth

So, I'm sorry

You will forever be missed
As I end this letter,
letting you rest in peace,
I seal it with a kiss.

Laurencia

Loving you was easy
It felt so right
Like it was meant to be
You completed me

Though we were on two different pages,
when we got back together,
Things were on
like shit never faded
Then you left with my heart
and nothing seemed right

The thought made me sick
knowing you were out of my life
Deep down, I was hurt
which for others, made me keep up my guard
It was because you had hurt me
The wound didn't heal
It always stayed open
There was no scar, and I was just hoping
I would overlook my feelings
and whatever I made up

Hell, that was the reason…
Actually, it was a reason…
You were the reason…
It was you that I wanted to be pleasing
All that is gone
because true love,
always finds its way back home,

Let's make a home; Our home
A family

Doesn't really matter to me
As long as I have you, I'm truly happy
I close my eyes
I see your unique complexion
Your beautiful smile
Your pretty eyes
I'm thankful that you are mine
These are the thoughts that I have of you
I know that it is fate and faith that has me with you
I love you so much
You're all I need in this world
I love you, forever, my girl

Ebony

We walked by each other countless times
A *hello* here or there
But no serious conversations

Then one day, our friends found it interesting
To play matchmaker
Setting us up on a date
I didn't really care because
I didn't think it would go anywhere, anyway

"So, who do you plan on hooking me up with?"
Was the question I asked
They told me you,
Ebony Walker

I smiled at first, which turned into a laugh…

"There is no way that she would talk to me
We say hello but, that's about all…
Tell her if she is serious, here's my number;
Give me a call!"

Seeing you around was a little bit different now,
Because our eye-to-eye contact
Started with a smile

More words were said, as our conversation picked up
Phone calls were enlightening
as we talked from dawn to dusk
We began dating and I saw you in a different light
It was something about you
that I just adored,
You were down to earth, easy to talk to,

which I never really experienced before
Everyone noticed that us being together
was a great, unexpected thing
The happiness we had was more than just a fling

Days turned into weeks, as weeks turned into months
I was full of joy that I had you as my better half
It was like a rose that you watch bloom,
smiling, knowing that the end result of this beauty
could light up a room

Then one night,
things changed again
When you whispered in my ear that you loved me
You became SOMEONE SPECIAL
Not just my girlfriend

You cheered me on at football games
Picked me up for school
We walked around just talking,
clowning and being fools
I was hurt when you moved away
Though you were gone,
your love never went astray
It stayed in my heart forever,
where it still remains

Because the promise I made to you,
I will love you always,
was a promise that I just couldn't break
Holding you in my arms,
and just gazing into your eyes,
were priceless moments I loved
as time just flew by

You had my heart,
and that is something I hardly give to people
That's why I guess us talking again,
Is part two, the sequel

The feelings that I have,
I try hard to fight
You know how I feel,
I've always wanted you in my life
So, do I act on my feelings?
Sit back on my feelings,
Hear you out,
To react to these feelings?

I don't know, but this feels like a dream
Something I see…
Loving the sweet, beautiful you
Ebony

Ms. D. Jones

Even though you were older than me,
I would look at you and still think
That you were so beautiful
Yeah, you were a sister
to one of my friends,
but I still would wished
that I could kiss you
Just for pretend

Then I started getting older
and I would see you at school
with the older click
So, I laid back with my friends,
trying to be cool
Of course you didn't notice,
Actually, I didn't expect you to

The day you spoke to me
Was the day I really fell in love with you
Well, not really love;
I was just happy you spoke,
So happy, in fact
that I wrote you a note

I never gave it to you
because it didn't flow right,
I tried to get you out of my mind
I wanted to say hello to you,
but the words would never gel or mend
In my mind, we were lovely together
In reality, I couldn't comprehend

No, I wasn't a stalker

Nor was I crazy
Well, I was crazy about you
Daydreaming about you
Was the best thing to do
We're both older now
and my thoughts have matured
We've been through heartache
and bad situations,
but this is my cure
I still think about showering you
with a thousand kisses,
or telling you that you're my baby,
my sexy lady!

Show off my cooking skills,
Or write you a poem,
Showing you,
That I want to be with you

We may never do anything more,
than exchange pleasant phone conversations,
Meet up for dinner and a movie,
Looking at each other;
Contemplating…
Do we kiss?
hug,
hold hands,
cuddle and snug?
I wouldn't even know what to do,
I would just be happy being close to you

These thoughts cross my mind,
flowing deep to my bones,
because I don't know what I would say face-to-face
To the lovely Ms. D. Jones

What Obstacles?

I wonder what obstacles you all have to overcome,
to get to the point of where you are now
How many times did you make her cry or break a promise?
Break her heart?
What did you do to put a smile on her face?
Throughout the day,
Throughout the years,
As a couple,
What were your biggest fears?

You look at him and smile as if
he is the most beautiful thing you know...
How many times
have you falsely accused him of something?

Have you ever doubted that he truly loves you?
If you did, what did you do?
What did you say?
I can sit back and watch you two all day

I wonder what obstacles you all had to overcome
to be the loves of each other's lives
How did you maintain a healthy relationship?
When true love is so rare to find

As you look into her eyes, and say *"I love you"*
and ask her, *"Do you love me?"*
She replies with a *"yes"*
A part of me is jealous because
I've been searching and looking for something
that you all have and it's so precious
Like a diamond in the rough
What did you all do when the times got tough?

You let her walk up some, as you fall back,
And bend down and grab some of the Fall leaves
That are on the ground
As soon as she turns around,
You hit her in the head with them,
But, you slip down
You're both laughing
To my surprise, she lays on top of you and kisses you
She then gets up and helps you stand
Like little kids playing in the sand

I'm in total shock
that this elderly couple, holding hands at the park
is so vivid and alive
They have so much love and imagination
I sit on the bench just looking at you both,
Enjoying the time…
Enjoying the moment...
Enjoying each other

As I sit and wonder what obstacles you all
had to overcome,
it simply doesn't matter
because whatever the obstacle was,
it didn't affect the love that you two have for each other

I learned a lesson without saying a word,
sitting and observing an elderly couple
having so much fun

No matter what obstacles arise, as long as you have love,
commitment and trust,
everything will work itself out

My Morning with My Favorite AKA

After a wonderful encounter with you,
I'm looking forward to this evening
You have been on my mind
All day
The flow is smooth
So I go along
with what we have developed

Text messages
Just to let each other know
that we are being thought of
I can't help but to keep thinking
about the soft lips that you have
When you placed that kiss on my cheek,
your beautiful face was the last thing
I envisioned before I went to sleep

Now, you have me smiling
because we both know that we are going
to see each other tonight,
and I'm looking my best,

All I want to do is be with you
I'm not moving fast,
but I know that you are leaving soon,
so I want the memories to last

Change of plans
I won't be seeing you as anticipated
I'm kind of upset and a little devastated,
but you tell me to meet you at your room instead
Now I'm elated

The night is coming to an end,
At last…
I'm on my way to see you,

You open the door slowly
I have the biggest smile on my face,
because I've finally made it to your place
Couldn't wait
to hold you in my arms,
Kiss you slowly
with my hand around your waist
All day I've waited for this exact moment,
For us to be face to face,
but the more I try to let the words out,
I'm speechless
My heart is beating at such a rapid pace

Conversation has ended
and now I'm kissing those lips,
While I feel you in my arms
grinding those hips
Your hand is on my face,
And I'm kissing on your neck,
working my way down
from your lips,
to your sweet "Cami Cake"

Gently…

I kiss both sets of lips,
The rolling of your eyes has me turned on
I wasn't picturing this
But, since we are at this moment,
I'm going to enjoy it

Sit you on my lap,
Kiss you slowly again
My hands are all over your back
Though I want you to lay back,
I get a thought in my head
that is sure to make you react

I pick you up
and see the surprise in your eyes
Don't even trip,
or be fooled by my size

On to the bathroom sink,
Kiss you slow,
Followed by a sexual wink,
Licking and kissing your lips,
Are we about to do what I think?
Yep,
it's going down,
more like it's going in
and you breathe hard with a smirk,
followed by a grin

One hand is in my dreads,
Tilted to the side is your head
The other hand is on the faucet
The more I look at you,
The more I can't stop it
Deep strokes, followed by passionate kisses
You are as soft as I imagined

I'm wishing this moment will never end

We have pulled an all-night, unexpected bedroom scene
I'm not the one, but, right now
it would feel even better
if you were sleeping next to me
You grant my wish
While we lay in each other's arms
The morning is complete
Your body is so warm
I can't sleep
I just watch you at peace

I'm trying to figure out what's wrong
This is unlike me
To let somebody get close
I don't know what it could be
Then I just think that this was pure
No gimmicks or strings attached,
Truly sincere

We have something that others lack;
The sense of respect for each other

This came without a warning
Just watching you sleep in my arms,
Kissing you good night baby,
I can never forget
My unforgettable morning
I guess there is nothing left to say,
But, *"Thank you for a wonderful time"*
to my favorite AKA

I Don't Want to Go

I just sit on the bed for hours,
The thought of you no longer here
is simply tearing me up
At the same time,
it hasn't registered or hit me yet

The emotions that are going through me,
are unexplainable
I'm up and down,
I'm sad then crying
Then I get happy because
I know that you are in a better place

The quietness in the room
is actually making it harder to concentrate
My mind is in one place
While my heart is in another
The more I sit back and think,
I realize how selfish I was
for taking you and your presence for granted
The more I go in depth with my thoughts,
the more I can't stand it

So many times you just wanted to sit down,
Talk to me,
See how I was doing,
Or what was going on in my life;
I would ride
right by the house,
wouldn't even stop through to say *hi*
I'm into everything moving,
Now I'm in this room,
Emotionally dying,

Trying
Not to bring the guilt of pity on myself
Saying I'm sorry
Deep in my prayers is the time
That I'm talking to you
When the truth of the matter is
that I never really knew what to say

Your sickness had you in a different
State of mind
and I didn't want to see you like that
Okay, I'm lying
I couldn't stand to see the strong person
that I had seen throughout my life
In the condition that you were in!
It made me sick
It made me sad
I questioned so many times,
Why you?
That answer never came to me

So, I was even more outraged,
with anger and hurt
Writing you now is probably the hardest thing
I've ever done
because there are so many things that I want to say

My vision is constantly blurred
The tears I had to keep wiping away
I'm sorry
So sorry
that I didn't do more
and I just wanted to tell you that I love you
I'm going to miss you
Just as much as everybody else

You touched me in so many ways
and when you thought I was just this wild child
that went astray,
I saw the light that you were talking about
on that particular day

I'm sorry that I didn't always say the right thing,
or grasp the concepts of life that you were
trying to make me understand
when I had you right here
Everything was crystal clear
I just didn't open up my ears

I'm sitting up looking at this black suit,
black tie, black shirt, black belt,
black shoes
Constant knocks are at the door,
I just don't want to go to your funeral,
because I want to have my own personal time
and cherish these memories of you

Emotions from Elliot

I'm so hurt
It hurts to breathe
or even stomach the fact
that you and I will never be
more than anything
ever again

I call to talk to you
and you tell me
that you have a boyfriend,
and we can't talk anymore
Am I hearing this right?
Did you say what I think you did?
I have to be imagining things
This has got to be pretend
Because we promised each other
That no matter what,
we would always be friends!

I feel crushed
This is so personal
The love I have for you
is permanent and irreversible
I don't know if I want to scream
or even shout
My heart's been ripped out
Shattered...
Destroyed...
I can't get rid of this feeling
I can't get the hurt out of my heart
My emotions are all over the place,
I'm completely torn apart

How do I pick up the pieces
and love someone
the way that I loved you?
A true dilemma
I don't know what to do

I can't even lie
This hurts so bad
I want to cry
Just know that I will never love
anyone the same
I never dreamt or even pictured this
Feeling
of emptiness
without you

Trying to get closer,
Just to kiss you one more time
Seal the deal
For real
with closure
Now that you're gone,
I go to this place in my mind,
and think about you
As my thoughts are stuck in repeat,
replaying everything
about us,
over and over,
I know I have to accept the fact
that we are through
Nothing else to do
and the only things I can say is:
I'm sorry that it came to this,
but I'll always love you

Apology

I've waited for 3 years,
8 months,
a week and a half,
plus 2 days
for you to say
what you had to say
I'm feeling a whole lot better today
'cause the only way,
for us to be at this point
was for me to pray

We've finally cleared the air
Put our feelings on the table
about what was right and wrong,
what was fair and unfair

I don't want to look back
I just want to move forward
Our communication issues
always play a major factor
and sometimes it haunts us
I felt as if you ran from me,
knowing how tight we were
I had anger built up inside,
because I knew that I sincerely and genuinely,
apologized and wanted nothing but my friend back

You felt that you needed me and my help
and you were trying to figure out why I did
certain things as if I was running away
So, that's how you protected your feelings
But, you said that you wanted your friend back,
as well

I guess neither one of us knew how to be that
without all the emotions that were still tied
between us

This apology
was heartfelt
and it needed to be said,
but it needed to be said so long ago
It's better late than never, though

I never closed the door
on us finally sitting down and addressing,
what our real problems were
We have a wonderful, beautiful child together
It's obvious that we both love her,
always and forever
We just had our bumps and obstacles
that we needed to get over
so we could appreciate things more
while trying to figure one another out

Where you felt neglect,
I felt disrespect
By us communicating,
there's nothing but the highest admiration
for each other
Guess we still have those unique feelings
that are sometimes surreal

Thank you for this clarity session
I think we both have learned a valuable lesson
That communication is a key factor

I accept your apology

Lifetime Companion
(Thoughts of Randy Thomas and R.I.P Sherene)

Losing someone is hard,
especially a lifetime companion
My heart goes out to you…
For you,
I'm there
You're my friend,
and friends are there for each other
Our symbolic friendship is unique
So we are like brothers
That's why your pain is my pain

I've learned so much from you,
When I was off doing dumb things,
it was your voice in my head,
Thank you so much
You helped me change my ways
and my thoughts,
which led me to say
whatever fight that you had
is going to turn into a brawl,
an attention-grabbing moment
Pulled to the side,
I don't care what you all do,
Don't let anything happen to my baby!
As you replied…
Promise me
that as long as you are around,
you will always have Randy's back
I promise, Sherene
That's a fact

I was jealous
You had something that I wanted;
A lifetime companion,
Someone that you could grow old with
Make your wife,
and have kids
Then all of a sudden,
without any notice,
or warning signs,
your lifetime companion was gone

I wish I could bring back your happiness
The love of your life,
Your best friend,

My heart died when I heard the news,
So if it was hard on me,
then I know it was harder on you
Out of this tragic situation,
there's still sun light,
shining down on your life
You have your beautiful daughter Iyhana,
brightening things up for you

I look up to the sky,
tell Sherene there's no need to cry
Everything is okay
Everything is alright
We've reconnected our bond,
and together, we're back to doing,
big things again
So, I'm upholding my end of the bargain,
And I promise
To continue to be there for my lifetime friend

On This Day

On this day,
you came into my life
when everything felt so wrong
Opening up to you,
was oh so right
I didn't have any intentions
on letting you in my world
I mean, we were cool,
but I was dealing with so much turmoil

The more we talked,
The more I was at ease,
Thinking about you,
The more I was pleased

You gave me comfort and support,
which was something
that I was lacking
Before I knew it,
I couldn't believe what was happening

Yes, I was skeptical
Letting you in,
I had to keep thinking on it
Why?
I knew that you were something special
A day turned into two,
A week transformed into a month
It didn't take long;
I knew that I loved you

Now, we are here...
Months have turned into a year

Though we are not where we want to be,
I'm not going anywhere
I love you so much
Memories that we share,
I will never forget
You're my other half,
From childhood,
To us being grown
A different kind of love,
is something that you have shown

All my troubles
You seem to mend
That's what it is like
To have you as a best friend
We will have so many more memories
That will never fade away
But on this day,
You made me feel so special

Something so small and minor
turned out to be something big
Thank you for allowing me
To come inside your heart
From this day forth,
we will never be apart!
Sharing with each other,
Two have already become one
Our life together
has only just begun
So, the biggest thing,
That I really wanted to say,
is I'm glad you decided to
let me in your world, a year ago, today.

The Way Mommy Sees It

All the sucking your teeth
I want to hit you so bad
That's right,
Put my hands on you
You have me that mad
The more I listen to you,
The more I want to slap you!
Hard
Drop you to the ground

I'm looking up at the ceiling,
asking God for a double dose of strength

Working overtime
Then having to come home and deal with this mess
You're stressing me
Turning hairs on my head gray
Better yet,
Just walk away
Get out of my sight
Fast
Now
Go in the room,
Relax,
Chill out
No, matter of fact,
Let me go take a shower,
So I can calm down,
Get my thoughts together
We'll discuss things later
I need more time to figure out
What to do
What move to make

Be able to tell whether the truth is going to come out,
Or if a lie is going to push through
This uneasy uncertainty
actually has me spooked

The shower is off
Have the emotions settled now?
Hopefully so
In the room to talk sensibly,
We are going to hash out these situations
So, you need to speak truthfully
Don't look around dumbfounded,
Thinking of how to lie to me
And if you do,
I promise it's going to take
the angels of God
To pull me off of you

Hearing my mom talk like that
Let me further know
That I didn't want to be punished
I knew that angels
weren't just going to come down
and pull her off of me
Me messing up
was the consequence!
I had to take the beating;
But, to my surprise,
These words arised:
Go to your Aunt Linda's house,
And let her deal with you!
Thank you God for this breakthrough!
Aunt Linda isn't going to beat me,
Just preach to me for an hour or two;

So, I thought

Get to Aunt Linda's house,
Here comes the talk, but
Out of the blue
Aunt Linda tells me that she is going
to deal with me too
More like she is going to beat me
for my mom

We are going to hurry up,
and get this over with
and I'm going to let you get back along

Aunt Linda beat me for about
two to three minutes
It happened so fast
I couldn't believe Aunt Linda
Was beating my…
Ask
No questions
Don't even make any comments
If your mom tells me that you
have been acting out again,
there is going to be a serious problem

That's not a problem I want to have
Aunt Linda beat me so quick and fast
that once I got home to my room,
I had to laugh
It really wasn't funny,
But, it was a comical moment

Mommy asked me if Aunt Linda had beat me
Yes ma'am, she did

So, because she thought I was lying,
she called my aunt to confirm
Aunt Linda told her that she did in fact beat me
Mommy couldn't believe it
She never thought her sister would see the situation
the way she sees it

Hello Cold Cruel World

Here's looking at you…

Mixed-Up Feelings

I can't keep fighting these feelings that I have for you
Sometimes, it bothers me...
Stresses me...
I don't know what to do

Am I coming or going?
The tension is thick
I try to be so cool,
but at times you make me sick
To my stomach,
through to my bones
I want to distance myself,
but we can't leave each other alone

Being with you is an emotional rollercoaster
A natural disaster
We're trying to hold on to something
Is it really worth reaching?
I feel like this situation we are in
is a puzzle that we are trying to put together
with a million pieces

You're ready to leave
Hell, I'm ready to ride,
Neither one of us wants to make a move
I guess it's the pride
Then I see that look in your eyes
Saying: *"Baby, hold on! Our love is worth the try."*

I don't even get caught up in the emotions
I just calm down to avoid the commotion

I feel like I cheat myself,
More like cheating my feelings
Like they've been kidnapped
and I'm holding them for ransom
For the right price, I'll let them go for the passion

I don't know what to do about us
I love you so much
But honestly speaking...
that's not always enough

My soul is outside,
and my heart needs serious healing
I'm tired of suffering
from these mixed-up feelings

Breakups

This breakup is hard
It's intense and sickening
I'm exhausted and drained,
My thoughts are constantly shifting
I can't focus on things
My mind is always drifting
My heart is ripping
emotions sifting
I'm trying to piece it all together
I can't!
I feel myself sinking...
Drowning...
In misery

The heartache is unbearable
Thought we would always be together
I thought we were inseparable
This breakup is hard
My emotions are out of whack,
'cause the truth of the matter is
I just want you back

I know that will never be
An "Us"
or a "Together"
A "You and Me"

My vision is blurry
You're fading and being erased
from my memory
I don't want to eat
My appetite is gone

I just lay in the bed,
looking at the ceiling,
trying to figure out
where I went wrong
I try working
just to get me through
But I always catch myself thinking of you

Moving on is the hardest thing to do
but it's necessary
So you can get on with your life
I'll keep progressing too,
letting time heal these scars

One Way Conversation... Pt. II

I just walked through door
from a long day, but a very interesting night
The information I received
has me contemplating a different outlook
of changing my life
Not just my life; our life

I walk down the hall calling out your name
So I can share this feeling
that has been driving me crazy
with you
You come from the room and slam the door abruptly
"What's wrong with you baby?"
I see this look in your eyes
I know something is wrong, because that look,
you can't hide

"Where have you been? What have you been doing?"
I open my mouth to respond,
but before a word comes out,
you yell FUCK!
I'm looking at you like what?
You say, "I saw you at the bar, talking to that slut!"
"Baby, hold on! I can explain that,
let me explain what happened!

But, you aren't letting me get a word out to talk,
You slap me in my face over and over, repeatedly!
So, before things escalate any further,
let me chill out and just walk.

Where the hell you going now?
To go be back with that bitch?

Fuck you punk, because you think you slick!

I haven't done anything,
you're taking what you saw out of context,
This isn't what you think
Shut up! I don't want to hear nothing
you are trying to say
I saw that bitch you was talking to in pink

Baby, if you stop over talking me, I can explain...

You are so mad, your response is whatever,
and you're just wasting your breath
I try to reach out to you, just to let you know
what you thought you saw, wasn't true

No, I saw what I saw, you're just trying to run game
And trying to lie right in front of my face
is a low down dirty shame
You always talking about you working late,
when you really out playing
I work hard for me! For us!
I gave you the world, and put up with
all your bullshit,
And this is how you do me,
I can't believe this

If you would please be quiet
and let me speak for just one minute,
I can explain the whole situation

And after you have heard my side of the story,
you can determine for yourself,
if I'm really playing
Please! Just leave

because the sight of you is making me
hate you right now
I swear

I'm nauseous and sick
I can't even believe that you aren't even
trying to hear me out right now
Please, shut up and go!
Before I do something regret
I'm hot as hell, and I'm starting to sweat

Fine have it your way, I'm about to be out!
I'm not in the mood to scream and shout,
You have put up with my shit,
and been there from the jump
I wouldn't do you any ole kind of way,
and do any of that stuff!
When you're ready to talk,
you know how to contact me

I can't even believe this shit
I haven't done anything wrong
Tension is thick,
Grab my cell phone to call my boy, Demetrius

Dee, I've got something to tell you
I'm on my way over to your house
We got into it again
You really aren't going to believe this shit!

Meanwhile, I'm looking back at you,
With you saying:
Yeah, whatever just leave,
leave me alone, and I mean that shit

Nicole (Vengeful Somber)

I can't believe this guy isn't showing any shame!
Thinking I'm dumb as hell,
some random chick off the streets,
I'm tired of these stupid games,
I want so much more,
And I want it with him
God, please enlighten your child with some insight,
from within
I saw both of them, with my eyes
Not what someone told me
I saw it
See it

He knows my history
He knows that I have been through this shit before
He must be a fool to think I will go for this drama
His ass will definitely be out the door
This is why I hear women scorned say
Get over on them before
They fuck over you

Then the shit won't hurt as bad
Now, I'm thinking to myself,
when you find out the truth,
This dumb ass is still trying to express and explain
My mind has drifted off,
now he sitting here complaining
Rattling and rambling on

I love when they try to flip the script,
and try to play victim
I've played the victim for years baby
I definitely didn't think I would have to play it with you

Now it's time to play the villain

He doesn't have sense enough to know
His own boys have tried to get at me and holla
I haven't said anything about it
Kept the thoughts in my mind
Like, these are who you call your friends,
They just like the company
and business people you keep
Going along for the ride
Trends
Been approached by other men,
Who trying to give up a dollar
Been hooked by bait
a couple of times or two
Fuck the bullshit
Time look for something new,

Now, I'm really thinking hard to myself
I 'm still thick and sexy,
whether he knows it or not,
As I smile

Hair and nails on point
I stay in somebody's shop,
Hit the gym on a daily basis
Trying to stay fine for you
But your ass stay in these bitches' faces
Now I'm completely numb
Can't hear a word you are saying,
I feel my mind being soothed
from thoughts of me doing the playing

Plotting and scheming,
You have given me the reason

Starting with Demetrius
He is such an easy target
I see the way he looks at me
I'm kind of wrong,
but, in my mind, I'm thinking,
If I give him this pussy one good time,
that will be the beginning of something sweet
Who cares that they are best friends
Pussy always settles the score
Anyway, I'm about to exit this 'one way conversation',
But you exit stage left,
and slam the fucking door

Demetrius (Cold Hearted Illuminations)

Just got the call, Nick and Slim
Man my homeboy heading over
They at it again
Probably something this dude did
I'm not going to take sides
Just listen
and be a supportive friend

He says he met his cousin at a bar,
then out of nowhere, his girl walked up on him
Now she's at the crib popping off
Yeah, in this situation he was probably right,
but because of all the other shit he's done
that's probably what led to this fight

That dude can mess up if he wants to
I mean yeah,
He is my friend and all
but if Nicole needs a shoulder to cry on,
I know it's going to lead to some other shit

Me on
Her
I'm bugging out hard

Payback and revenge is best served cold
Let me pour my ass another drink

Got to sit here and listen to him whine and complain
I'm sorry man
All this back and forth isn't that serious
Most of them want you to feel guilty anyway
That shit ain't nothing but a marriage trap
I don't have time to listen to the rambling
I just hope he slips up one time,
so I can see if she is really that thick

This dude is a trip
Here we go with the squandering and revelations
I can tell from how things sound
Right now, it's about to be a one-way conversation

Knocks at the door
Damn, he's here
Let's get this over and done with

(A Couple hours later...)

I've vented to Demetrius
I feel a whole lot better
Just to get things off of my chest,
Have someone listen to me, and not really judge
The more it sinks in,
The more I think
Man, this is unbelievable

I'm sitting in the driveway,
Thoughts are delusional and sideways
Actually,
this is all too funny
and when the truth comes out,
you are going to be looking like a dummy

I can't take this anymore
As I walk into the house,
you still have this twisted demented look
And before a word comes out,
I put my hands over your mouth,
Tell you there are some things you need to hear,
So, before you pass judgment,
here's to settling the mood
And clearing the air

See, what I wanted to tell you was
Yeah, I did meet a chick at the bar,
but it was my cousin
I told her to meet me because I needed her opinion
Something was on my mind and I needed her
to help me with a decision

You woke me up one morning,
telling me about this dream
So I had my cousin go with me to make your
dream come true, and surprise you
with an engagement ring
I wanted a female's perspective,
and point of view
of how something so beautiful
would look good on you

I didn't think that you would come to the spot
where we hang out
So, I'm wrong because in a sense, I did cover the truth
But, I wasn't doing anything wrong,
That's just what happens
when you get this perceived notion
and start to assume
Leading to a typical one-way conversation

Just Asking (Pt. I)

I'm tired of all these changes,
All these phases...
I'm tired of the BS
And the crazy situations

I think that it would be best
If I left
Us together,
is bringing nothing but stress
My tank is on empty

Every time I try to talk to you,
It's followed by a smart remark,
and it's things like that,
tearing us apart
Hectic
Even drastic
That's why I'm saying I need a break
Because I simply can't stand it

It's not me walking away,
but I'm taking a breather
So I can get my thoughts together,
and see things clearer
I don't like to clash
Arguing and fighting
It's just not me
That's why I try to be the bigger person
So, we can make things last
But all I get
is your ass
to kiss,
So I'm out

I mean that shit
I know that relationships
have their ups and downs,
but it's not fair that you try
to run me into the ground

Is this going to last?
I don't even feel like
this is a question I should ask
Then again,
Yes, I do
I need that answer out of you
I need you to be truthful

There are so many things
going on in my mind
and at this present time
I don't think it'll all be fine
I don't want to keep feeling like
something is lacking
So, you need to let me know what's up,
because I'm tired of asking

To Be Continued...

It took me a while to open my eyes
and realize just how closed-minded
you really were
A lot of things you say and do
are so unfair,
but throwing you under the bus,
I wouldn't dare

Let's get to the real root of the matter
Instead of you accepting situations,
for what they are,
you constantly keep trying to change things
If it doesn't feel right to you,
then there's always something wrong
with me for expressing myself
the way I know how to

I don't always like going to your parents' house,
Not that it's anything wrong with going over there,
but those are your parents;
Not mine
And because I don't let you in my world,
you're quick to say that there is something that
I'm trying to hide

Honestly,
I'm not hiding anything
I just don't talk to you because regardless
of the conversation,
you always have a comment,
and there are times when I need you to be
my friend and just listen

Not be so judgmental
about how I need to forget and forgive,
because it's not always that simple

You haven't gone through what I have
and instead of you constantly
clashing with me,
maybe you should think about
why I'm being the person
that I appear to be

Talking to you doesn't get me anywhere,
but back to sly comments
and subliminal insults
So, why bring you around
to meet my friends and do things
that I like to do,
which is comfortable to me,
but clearly not to you

Because I don't agree to your terms,
I'm not trying to make a change
you're quick to point out my flaws
and my faults,
from the way I dress
to the way that I talk
I'm not going to apologize

I said all of that to say
that I'm not really the selfish person
in this equation
Maybe you would see that if you looked
further into this situation

I told you everything that was going
to take place before it even happened,
Now you're acting as if those conversations
Never occurred
You're so moody,
it's hard for me to be myself around you
It's like a burst of sunshine
transforming into an immediate gray cloud

Now, you might think that I'm saying this because
I don't care,
but that is the total opposite
If I didn't care,
I wouldn't be saying any of this
I'm just trying to shed light
on a dark moment right now,
Wishing some way or somehow,
Things can change immediately
So, it's all on you
Until then,
I'll leave this to be continued…

Listen

Listen,
Your mind is so far gone
You're not mine,
and we're not together anymore
I hope you get the picture,
That you're not what I want
and I can't say it any clearer

You're trying to pry,
and figure out what I'm doing,
Who I'm screwing
or possibly pursuing
I'm not worried about you,
So, don't worry about me
I'm not trying to be mean,
I'm just enjoying life

You don't have to come by
with the trench coat
with the bra and panty set on
I don't even see you like that
So, you can leave me alone

You think because you look good,
that's going to get you by
Sorry, I'm not interested,
so find another guy
that will follow your reply,
your every command,
Sit when you tell him to sit,
and stand when you tell him to stand
I'm my own man

This has gone on long enough,
and I'm tired of talking
Lose my number,
Stop the stalking
Be gone
Hell,
Be out
Out of my life,
Out of my system,
You're
Out of control

Listen,
I'm not reacting to you
or any of the things you say,
nothing that you do
Open your eyes…
Surprise!
My memory has erased
you out of my life

Seeing You

I said that I wouldn't know how to react
if I ever saw you face to face
Perhaps, I would smirk
Maybe I would laugh
Us crossing paths
You would feel my wrath
Man, kiss my ass
Naw, that's my inner thoughts,
just talking out loud
I wouldn't give you the satisfaction,
or the pleasure of getting aroused
Knowing that you're getting under my skin
is something that will never happen again

That day has arrived
Actually, I'm surprised
We make eye-to-eye contact,
You're opening your mouth
like you're about to let something flow out
I'm shaking my head no; please don't go that route
Don't make me embarrass you for speaking
Silly rabbit,
What are you thinking?
Knowing me, I would say hello
and you would be shook,
acting real shallow
You wouldn't know which direction to take
I'll be laughing inside
Yep… Checkmate!

With all that said,
the best thing to do is to just keep walking,
like I don't even know you

When It Comes

I know everything about you,
from your smile,
down to your smirk
When you are upset,
In a good mood,
Or your feelings are hurt
I value your worth,
and try to show you
my love is real

Our love has developed
and grown stronger,
as we matured,
from kids to adults
See, when it comes
To you
I know you like
the back of my hand
When no one can figure
you out,
it's funny to me
because you are easy
to understand
I had the master plan,
but we both got sidetracked

Loved each other,
Hated each other,
Been apart,
Trying to decipher an
Unsolved mystery
that has brought
us back together

When it comes to you,
You can say whatever
you want
The truth is always
in your eyes
No matter how hard
You try
To hide
What you feel
Your eyes never lie

Now, this may come as a surprise
Hopefully, you realize
That
When it comes to you,
I have your ways down pat
I know you like I know
None other
The relationship we have is so strong,
It makes me wonder
How did it even get to this point?

When it comes to you
I'm not scared to tell you
That I love you

Bad Habits

Everything is fine and cool
This is not the time
To show me the good side of you
I want to know what your
Bad habits are
Are you down to earth?
Are you lazy?
A psycho chick?
Or are you half crazy?

Do you make strange noises
When you're tired or sleepy?
Would you go through my phone,
texts, or emails?
Are you sly and sneaky?

I'm slick at the mouth,
And when I'm mad,
I'm far from calm
I tend to stutter,
get teary eyes,
And have sweaty palms
I keep quiet,
and seldom communicate
for me to come out of my shell,
I'm sorry, but you will just have to wait

I'm not saying that this is how I'll be forever,
I'm just saying that these
are some of my bad habits

I just bring them to the forefront
So that when you do see them,

You won't end up snapping
I bite my nails,
When I'm thinking or nervous
Sometimes I'm nonchalant,
and I can be overzealous
I clean a lot,
I'm far from jealous

These are just some bad habits,
That I possess,
Whatever yours are,
Honestly, I could care less
as long as we are trying to better ourselves
and you're not into starting mess,
things will be fine
We can definitely progress

So tell me,
what are some of your bad habits?

Lost Wife

I've been at work all day
Holding it in
Not bragging or boasting
I couldn't wait to come home to you
To tell you about my promotion
Left early,
Thoughts of you were on my mind
We've struggled long enough,
With this promotion, we will be fine

Coming around the corner,
Pulling up to the driveway
Man, whose Tahoe is this
all in the way?
Whatever, it doesn't matter,
That's what I tell myself
Anxious to see you
And nobody else

Open the door, and to my surprise,
My house is quiet
Something's not right...

I'm downstairs looking for you
From room to room,
I have the Champagne bottle in my hand,
and
I'm ready to celebrate
I go upstairs to find you,
I can hardly wait
To tell you about my day
and give you the good news
Let you know that we can finally do

All the things we want to do
I come by our room,
Hear the water running
Which lets me know you are in the shower
Then, I hear you mumbling
Are you on the phone?

The closer I get,
The more your words are clearer
Saying, "I miss you so much"
"I want you nearer"

Who are you talking to?

I walk into the bathroom,
Look in the shower
and it's another dude
We're all surprised
I've got hurt in my eyes
I'm so crushed, and can't even fake it
Now, I'm swinging and fighting,
While y'all are both butt naked

Emotions are all over the place,
I'm completely devastated
I'm dragging this dude,
You got your hands around my hips
Man, get the hell off of me,
You trifling, cheating chick!

Reach for my gun,
'Cause I'm going to empty this clip
You're crying so hard
Saying don't... don't do this shit!

Arguing with you,
and dude gets away!
You're trying to talk,
There's not much you can say
I don't want to hear anything
That's about to come out of your mouth
Pack all your stuff,
Get the hell out of my house!

I sacrifice
To give you your wants, plus your needs
And this is the down-low thing
you decide to do to me?

You've let me down!
Can you tell me why,
After all I've done?
For you,
And us,
I can't believe you violated
Our bond
Our trust!
To think that I was trying to rush home,
To share my news with you
and you're here creeping with some other dude

Now, it's clear
That was his Tahoe truck,
I think you should call him,
And tell him to help you get your stuff!
Me and you
In this house together,
that can no longer be

I don't believe in divorce,
but this situation has changed my mind

Why?
I don't want to know!
You've broken my heart;
I feel it shattering to my soul,
From my head to toes
My best day has turned into disaster
How do I pick up the pieces
From this aftermath?
I don't know which path
To cross
Which direction to take!
I'm so hurt,
I'm irate!
There aren't enough sorries
That can make me change my mind!
With time, I will be fine...

Right now,
all I feel is hate!
Rage
I'm on a rampage!

Damn it
These feelings
I can't stand it
I can't take it
Shake it...
Hide it...
I can't even sleep.....
I'm up all times of the night,
Crying

How did I lose my wife?
Was it something I did?
I try to piece things together,
To make myself comprehend
I was a good dude,
And this is the result at the end
I'm tired of the pain and misery,
I just can't believe that you did this to me
I know that I have to move on with my life
but I'll forget the day
That I lost my wife

Kiss Me Goodbye

Kiss me goodbye,
Tell me that it's over
So we both can move on,
And end this with closure
We may be past our season
This break up was inevitable
And we already know the reason
Once again, I've given you a piece
of me, but
It's always the same outcome
You doing something dramatic
and making me feel ashamed,
mad, dumb

Kiss me goodbye
there's no need to be upset,
Just know that nothing will
ever be said, if we ever
Cross paths again
It's just that I can't
Keep giving you my heart,
And letting you rip it
In two,
Into...
A thousand pieces
Battering
and shattering
the blood out of me,
like a thousand leaches
Kiss me goodbye
and just know that we are through,
'cause the fact of the matter is
there is no more me and you

Missed

I miss the talks that we would have
Where we would just be up
All night long,
Laughing and playing, enjoying
Each other's company

No cares in the world,
but each other's initial feelings
I miss being able to hold you
In my arms and actually
Getting lost in your eyes for hours
Without one word being said,
Or us just jumping in the car
And taking a late-night trip
To the beach
Playing in the sand,
While we act like two of the biggest kids

I miss how the communication
Was so clear,
Crystal
Whatever plans we decided on
Wishful,
Thinking
I'm just sitting back reminiscing,
About when things between us were
Unique and we were full of life
Now, we just go through the motions
Our conversations are in the pits
I love you,
but I never imagined things between us
Would end up like this

Looks are hateful,
Rolling of the eyes
We still get comments,
Such as, "Y'all are cute together!"
But inside,
It is more like, "I can't stand you!"
What do we do?

How do we get the fire and flame back?
Because the harder we try,
The more we slack
The closer we get,
The further we take steps back

I miss meeting you in the kitchen,
Watching you cook,
Or kissing you and putting you on the countertop,
We are…
Well,
We were
So close
Now, we don't even get next
To each other

I'm just trying to get the "miss" factor
Out of our life,
and make it a reality again

There are times when I have to remind myself
That me and you were the best of friends
I miss sitting on the couch
Talking about our problems,
Trying to figure them out
If it was too stressful,

We were together
figuring it out
I guess in the end,
You think about the beginning

I miss all the wonderful times,
That we shared

I look you in your eyes,
Telling you that I never imagined things
would be like this,
and slowly walk away
From kissing your lips,
Thinking to myself;
You'll never know how much
you will be missed

Passing By

My heart is crying,
Along with these tears
From my face
For so long,
I've wanted you
I disliked you,
I hated you
Now, you are back in my life

I don't know
What to think
Or what to do
While my heart is crying,
It is uttering
My words are stuttering
As much as I love you,
I've wanted this moment
Forever
To make thing last
I'm truly sorry,
but our time has passed

It makes all the sense
In the world
To be with you,
but the pain from the past
Plagues me
there will always be discretions,
which isn't going to be
Fair to you

I say again:
I love you, I want you,

But, the pain
Won't let me follow through
I'm devastated emotionally
Full of scars,
And being with you is
Going to be too hard

Something's telling me to
Put the feelings aside
I'm so mad that you waited until now
To express how you feel
I really wish you could feel this hurt,
All the negative things that you said to me,
You worked nerves
In a horrible way
What more is there to say?
I don't know,
but as much as I love you,
My feelings for you,
Have faded away

My heart is crying,
Along with these tears,
From my face,
Feelings are dead and gone,
Though my love is strong,
It's just not enough,
For me to hold on
To you
It hurts me so
That I have to let you go
A head-on collision,
Disastrous crash
couldn't make things last;
I'm sorry, but our time has passed

Trust

I'm hurting so bad
It is all because of you
I turn my emotions off,
On to hating you
Not really hate,
but whatever is close to it,
that's how I feel
When it comes to you

The thought of you is making me sick,
Nauseous to my stomach,
Trying to vomit
You out of my system

The more I think of you,
The more I believe I'm jinxed
with this curse
of always getting hurt

I love too hard
So, that makes it much worse
And it's not just any chick,
It's you,
My so-called everything,
Trying to make dreams come true,
I'm through
Dealing with you

I said I would not go backwards,
To someone who makes my heart cold
And turns it blue
The more we try to evolve,
Seems like the more we dissolve

Like water evaporating
Into thin air
The way you have me feeling,
Is so unfair
I wouldn't dare
Put myself in a situation
where later,
It would be something
I would regret

The problem
We have is if the shoe
Was on the other foot,
I would be a dog,
No good,
Typical cheating guy,
but you act like because you apologize,
Everything is fine

I hear and accept your apology,
but the moment you told me,
That you entertained somebody else,
You lost a part of me

Can we ever get the trust back?
I guess time will tell
Right now,
I will tell
You
That I do still love you

I just can't trust you

Stalker

We cross paths
At a friend's party
Out of everybody,
You come and speak to me
The vibe that you are
Giving off is cool
We exchange numbers,
And begin to talk all the time
Even out of the blue,
You've stayed on my mind

We began seeing one another,
We haven't established a relationship,
but we are always there
for each other
I tell you to bring a bag
and stay the weekend at my house
Relax and chill
For this weekend only, you'll be my spouse

It sounded good
And I thought the plan was foolproof,
but you started doing some things
That I didn't expect you to do
Checking my voicemail,
Telling me that it needs to be "we"
That's not what I had in mind
And you're just here for a weekend
Everything in here is mine

Now, you can choose to leave,
Or chill out and unwind
Whatever route you decide,

Either way, I'm fine
I don't think what I said
Was all that bad or even hurtful,
but the things that I'm telling you,
are obviously bothering you,
I don't really understand why
But, you're ready to make things serious

I'm not running from commitment,
We're just really meeting each other
And rushing things so fast
Doesn't make sense
Now, the more we talk,
The more you get an attitude,
Because I'm busy
Or handling situations,
And really not including you

It's not that I'm keeping you
In the dark,
It's just there are some things that I do better,
When we are apart

I see where things are going
in this short amount of time,
And I haven't even made you mine
In my mind,
I don't need this stress,
I don't do drama

So, I'm telling you that I'd rather go my way
Than for you to think that I'm leading you on
Whether we get along,
Or don't ever talk again,
Wouldn't bother me, but

I would at least try to be friends
That sounds reasonable to me
Time has gone by,
yet some strange things stick out
Scratches on my truck
Emails that I haven't touched
are all of sudden read

Voicemail symbols on my phone after
an unknown call have disappeared
I'm scratching my head
You're the only one I know that would do such a thing

I pull up to my house,
put the key in the door
There's a necklace on the handle with a ring
and a note that reads:
I love you boo
There's food on the table and some outfits
on your bed that I bought for you

How did you get in my house?
Go to my truck, and take my pistol out
Call the police,
Tell them to get to my house quick
I can't even believe this
Walking around the house,
Like Martin and Will from Bad Boys,
I'm clutching the trigger,
Waiting for a unexpected noise
I hope this chick is inside

I don't know what to think

Police are here

Let me breathe easy
Tell them what's going on
They ask am I sure
I show them the note from the door
And tell them
That's all I have to go on
The officer informs me that I need a restraining order
And that you have stalker tendencies
This is crazy
I just wanted to chill out for the weekend,
but this is a weekend that I won't forget

Back to the work week
Enter my office and there are 12 long-stemmed dead roses
Scattered all over my desk
Is this happening again?
Police are at my job now
How did she even manage to make
it through security?
My team of co-workers,
Didn't see her come in
The more everyone talks,
I'm getting angrier because
She's like a ninja in the wind
I'm hoping that all of this
will soon come to an end...

Through a Text

Instead of telling me face to face
Or even over the phone
You send me a text message
Saying that you are upset
Fed up
That our lives are going in opposite directions
And that you need some time to just think
Things clearly through
Which is cool
But communicating feelings through a text message
Is something that I just wouldn't do
So, it kind of has me pissed off
Because I have to keep scrolling to see you
Get your feelings and point across

Though this is fixable,
Right now you make me sick
Not to the point where I want to lose you forever
It's just right now
The tension is thick
I thought we were better than this,
We are supposed to be each other's strength,
Where the other slacks
But, instead of telling me your feelings
You text me
So, what's going on with that?
Matter of fact,
I'll grant your wish,
And respect how you feel
I'll make myself and feelings clear
I don't want to lose you
I want you here
With me

Me without you
doesn't sit well with me
Get yourself together
Evaluate the situations
Take whatever political route you feel you need to
Go through the litigations
If the good outweighs the bad,
Then let's give it another try,
If not
I'll gladly leave
But, I'm stating my case for you right now,
With the highest respect
Because your love means that much to me
To tell you how I feel from the heart
Face to face
And not through a text

What Is It?

You want your cake,
Which is your husband
And you want to eat it too
Having me in your life as well
I can't be an option type person
If you had the feelings that you have,
Whether we were right or wrong,
We could have addressed them
Before you decided to get married
Now, you expect me to have all these feelings
That just aren't simply there
At all
Anymore

I guess me getting older has given me a sense
Of self-control
Because I wouldn't want my wife doing
Half of the things you do and say
And as much as I want to play
I have to say
No

I'm getting mad because if I said the things
To you that you say to me
Then it's the typical
"He isn't about anything"
"He's a dog or a cheater"
"I can't believe he's doing his wife like that"

So, if you think I'm going to give you
Any slack
I seriously doubt that

Now, don't get me wrong
We are cool and get along
But this is totally wrong

I have the mind frame to just
Tell you
That, yes, we are cool
But being caught in the middle of your emotions
Is just something that I can't do
I can't be a part of that
I'd rather eliminate myself
Completely out of the equation
Than to be in a possible situation
Or love triangle
I figured out the angle

I hate to lose our friendship
Me not being your only option,
But an option for anyone,
Is just something that I've never been
And I'm not about to start now
So, through all of those different emotions
I'd rather you leave me alone
Instead of allowing you
to keep leading me on

In the Morning

3:55 a.m. and I'm up
Mad as you know what
Ready to tear
This house apart
You're talking about me,
But you're the selfish one
How are you going to tell me that you want change
When you haven't changed yourself?

You want to point out my flaws
So let's flip the roles
I don't know what you were told,
But this being one sided and you acting like
You're the only one who has a say so
In a situation is not going to fly
And the more I try
The more I just want to give up

Comments that I'm "Hood" or "Ghetto"
Continue to come out of your mouth
Hell, when you show me the true definition of it
Make sure that you're able to
Point it out

I talk a certain way,
But I know how to adapt
To who is around and wherever I'm at
The more you speak with your close mindedness,
It makes me realize that there is something wrong
With you instead of me
You say that I'm ignorant
because I don't want to try new things,
but being with you is Déjà vu

I've seen this script played out the same way
With the same ending
You're talking like there's a child in here
And the things you're saying
I'm not comprehending

The more you talk,
The more you are digging your own grave
Guess that was "Hood" of me to say
Damn
Oh well
Right now, I don't even care
How you take what I'm saying to you
It's 3:55 a.m.
I should be sleep
Doing what normal people do

How Do I Move On?

My feelings are so strong,
I don't know what to do
How do I move on?
Stuck in the bed
Hanging on to the memories
And thoughts of you
Haven't shaved my faced,
Or even showered my body
How am I going to make it through?

My days seem meaningless
No care in the world
Just dragging along
My mind is stuck in misery
I don't know how to move on

My heart is in the pit of my stomach
I can't swallow or even digest
The emotions have me in this daze
I try to block out these feelings,
But somehow they remain

I try not to wear my emotions
All over my sleeves
The more I think of you,
I wonder what is wrong with me
The comfort you provided
Was so heartfelt and warm,
Is this why I'm at the stage
Of not being able to move on?

Days are short,
Nights are so long

Deep breaths and sighs
because the reality
Is that I need to move on
I have to move on…

Cards and memoirs
Pictures of you and us are gone
I'm still saddened by what
Has taken place
Certain songs make me remember
The beautiful smile on your face
I'm trying to put my heart
In a brand new place
It's so hard trying to be strong
Because without you,
How do I move on?

I'm the Reason

I'm feeling sad and down
I don't want to go out
I just want to stay at home
Turn off my phone
Just be left alone
You are so gone
And I need you here with me
My actions pushed you away

I've seen you many days and many nights
I didn't say anything
Just knowing that you were fine
Made me feel alright
Well...
It hurt me deep down so bad
Because I know I'm the reason
Why we are apart
It hurts my heart
Rips my soul
That you are gone
I want to hold and
Be held by you
But you hate me
Saying that I have the devil in me
And in hell
Is where I should be

So, this walk in a circle
In the bedroom
Has shown me the reality
That instead of being the man
I needed to be
You are gone

I'm the reason
And that's hard to deal with,
A tough pill to swallow
There's nothing left in me
Without you
I'm empty and hollow

Because of these broken bars,
I know you are gone astray
No reason for you to stay
Which hurts my heart
To know that I'm the reason
Why we are apart

Hurt

See what hurt the most
Was the hurt came from you
Everything you said
To everything that you would do
Made me shut down
Because I saw the look in your eyes
Everything we hoped for
Shriveled up and died

Instead of telling me
Where our flaws lay at,
I try to salvage what we have
You don't even react
You have given up on me
And my dreams
That's what it appears to be

So, you don't tell me,
Where we went wrong
Where my strong suits are
And where I slacked
The hurt that comes from you
Triggers my emotions

Yes, we have our ups and downs
That's expected in any relationship
We don't always agree with each other
On takes and outlooks
So things go wrong

I can't change any of your past hurts
I wish that I could
Because if I had the power to do it

You know that I would
But that doesn't change the fact
That you have given up on me
So it hurts a thousand times more
That I have to let you be

The love will always be there
That's something that won't change
And I'll keep doing what I do
So that I can maintain

I'll keep you off my mind
And bottle up my hurt
Because this pain
Has helped me
To finally see what I am worth

Pure Corruption

You don't know anything about me
You ramble and assume
I sit back and watch you
The alcohol, you consume
Then you transform into this
Horrific being
That I've never seen
Nor care to meet

All you do is down me
Tell me I will never amount to anything
Sorry
I will be successful
I will never accept defeat

You don't support me
Do you even know that sports are
My way of dealing with stress?
Despite all the horrible things
That you say and do
I'll always love you
But being caught up in your misery
Is something that I can't do

I watch you grab needles
Inject the poison in your arms
No matter how good it makes you feel
It's all just so wrong
At times I want to kill you
Because you hurt me deep down inside
The violence you portray
makes me want to run hide

Want to cry
and die

Truth of the matter is I hate you
I don't want to be anything like you
I try to get you help
I thought you would accept my plea
You didn't do anything
But laugh at me

You crushed my heart
I see that you don't care
I hate when you are on drugs
To me, it's so unfair
You don't know anything about me
Because your mind is corrupt
I guess that's why we don't share
Anything in common
And don't talk that much

I learned how to deal with the pain
To this day you are the reason
Why I've never thought about doing any drugs
Seeing what they did to you
Was something I was scared of

I hope this message
Finds its way to your heart
Because you are the reason
My life is torn apart

So Wrong

You are so sexy
I'm lying next to you
Admiring all of your curves
What feels all so right
Is all so wrong
I can't be with you
because I have a girl
I love her so much
Even though she gets on my nerves

What am I'm doing here
With you?
For a mere couple hours of pleasure
My pride and this pressure
Kissing me all over,
The feeling, I can't measure

I've already betrayed the trust
because of a fat ass and a pretty smile
I'm envisioning us
Butt naked, however it goes down
Seduced by lust
The more this goes on,
The more I'm crushed

I know I'm so wrong
My emotions are all over the place
Your breasts are all over my face
My hands all on your waist
What am I doing at your place?

I push her to the side
You are all that's on my mind

I've messed up, but I need to make things right
I see you
You roll your eyes of course
I'd rather make this work,
Then file for divorce
I reach for your arm
To get your attention
All I see is tears in your eyes
You tell me that you are tired of the hurt
And you are sick of the lies

If this divorce is what I really want,
Then you are ready to sign
I've tried to talk to you so many times
There's nothing but arguing and fighting
Slick comments and insults
Bickering and cussing
Slamming door
Ignoring each other or fussing

Even with all of this confusion,
The thought or illusion…
Losing….
You
I can't come to those terms

I look at you
As I take a deep breath
I swallow my pride
Look you in the eyes
I've cheated and I've lied
As I reply
There's nothing that I can say
To take back the hurt the pain
And all the times that I've made you cry

Even though you hurt me
Two wrongs don't make a right
I don't know how to make things right
But I had to get it off my chest
Because if we do part ways,
There will be no regrets

There's no logical reason,
For the things that I've done
And no matter how much
I try to justify things
I still know I was wrong

You look at me
And tell me that you respect
What I've said
And that you have violated our bond
By being in someone else's bed
You don't love him,
But you got caught up in the emotional feelings
And all the things he was saying

When I needed to be home,
I was hanging out all night
You told me it wasn't right
because I have a family and a wife
I didn't even see it like that
I can't even lie
The more you speak from the heart,
The more I see you're right

My party ways caught up to me,
Cost me my wife and my family
So, with all that said,
What do we do?

She tells me that as bad as I have hurt her,
Losing me
Is something that she doesn't want
I feel the same way

Whatever it takes to build our trust,
I'm willing and accepting
We will use this as a lesson
To keep our lines of communication open
So we won't be wondering or focusing
On things that we don't need

We got caught up for all the wrong reasons
But our love survived and overcame
A tragic situation
I'm sorry that I was hindered by attraction
I'm even more sorry that I became a distraction
I love you so much
Thank you for overlooking our faults
When times got tough

About the Author

Author Etrec J. White creatively uses his initials to describe himself as *Expressive, Jocund,* and *Witty.* He's been writing since age 9, inspired by personal life events and often pulling topics from random discussions.

Writing became a constant outlet once he realized his potential during English class in 4th grade. Etrec's teacher, Mrs. Searsy, complimented him on his beautiful handwriting and challenged him to write a short story. After completing the assignment, his work soon began to speak for itself, revealing hidden emotions and eventually allowing him to confront fears and express himself in a way that was uncommon to those he knew.

With his daughter as his muse, Etrec bravely addresses every challenge with his pen and his faith. This is his second collection of poetry, but with over one thousand poems already written, there's definitely more to come.

www.ingramcontent.com/pod-product-compliance
Lightning Source LLC
Chambersburg PA
CBHW031518040426

42445CB00009B/285